100 Keys To Love

Vicki Bennett

We acknowledge the Traditional Owners of the land on which we publish books, the Quandamooka people and pay our respects to Elders, past, present and future.

Published by:
Boolarong Press
38/1631 Wynnum Road
Tingalpa Qld 4173
Australia.
www.boolarongpress.com.au

First published 2022

A catalogue record for this book is available from the National Library of Australia

ISBN: 9781922643377 (paperback)

Typeset by Boolarong Press in Granjon LT Std 12pt
Set of vintage golden skeleton keys by Chones/Shutterstock.com
Cover design by Boolarong Press

Printed and bound by Watson Ferguson & Company, Tingalpa, Australia

Introduction

100 Keys to Love is about the yearning in each of us for connection with that one extraordinary person and the options available to us to make this happen. I interviewed hundreds of people for this book and found that we are not alone, each one of us is searching for love and self-discovery. Some people I spoke with have over-achieved in several areas of their lives but have felt frustrated about how to find love and happiness; a successful head-of-department of a high school was completely at a loss about how to sustain a healthy relationship with her partner.

Life is challenging. We are expected to work, be perfect mothers and fathers, sons and daughters, friends and lovers. Calmly juggling everything, balancing our lives, whilst looking fabulous.

Even with these challenges, it's an exciting time for humankind; so many opportunities, so much knowledge, and information is accessible. We have more choice and opportunity in education, careers, partnership, and the way we raise our children. Our voices are being heard globally, and we are connecting more with other communities. But when it comes to love we struggle to find it, express it, keep it, or untangle from it.

Human beings are optimistic, pessimistic, funny, troubled, enthusiastic, unsure, hilarious, kind, angry, disappointed, confident, shy, happy, sad, and joyous. But most of all curious — about our lives, about possibilities and choices for the future. This book offers choices for love, discovery, and change for those who are ready.

Each chapter is part of a knowledge map, giving direction and guidance to assist you in your journey of love. The messages in each chapter are aimed at creating a positive and productive mindset, offering ideas for loving and living effectively.

My deepest thanks to all the people who contributed to this book.

Vicki Bennett

Contents

Authentic Love

Authenticity is a collection of choices that we have to make every day. It's about the choice to show up and be real. The choice to be honest. The choice to let our true selves be seen.

Brené Brown

1.

Romance and love

There is something special about the romance that comes with falling in love. Opening your heart to another person can be thrilling and also terrifying at the same time.

It is completely normal to second guess yourself on your journey to find and accept love. Stay centered and as calm as you possibly can, so you can enjoy the experience.

Falling in love is exciting, exhilarating, and perhaps very new. It can also be unsettling because it asks for trust and a deep level of sharing. It can alter the way you manage your life; taking you into new, unchartered territory.

Enjoy these emotions and thoughts; it's a unique time in your life. Let your whole being enjoy the beauty of romance and love.

2.

Genuine love

It's natural to look forward to being in love but unrealistic expectations can change how you act with another person.

Keep the goal of romance in your mind but don't spend too much time thinking about it, or changing your natural way of being. Sending the wrong signals about your needs and wants makes it difficult to be seen and liked for who and what you are. If you don't act in your natural way, you will make it harder to attract genuine love.

Keep the door open for romance, but don't look at every person you meet as a possibility. Don't focus just on a romance, or finding that one right person. Be yourself and allow love to find you.

Let friendship and romance develop naturally.

3.

Perfect love

Falling in love is an incredibly special feeling but it's never going to be perfect.

Much is talked about romance as being the expression of perfect love, but having that special feeling all the time is not possible. Someone else can't make you happy all the time, just as much as you can't make someone else happy all the time. We are human after all.

You will be disappointed if you search for the perfect love, where the other person is thinking and caring about you constantly.

Because your heart will be excited and your hopes will be high, it's easy to lose your sense of reality by believing in this perfect love. If you can accept that love isn't going to be seamless all the time, then you will have a chance of finding lasting love.

Kind and gentle self-care is essential when falling in love. Generate good feelings about yourself and nurture yourself. If you care about yourself as much as you care about the other person, then falling in love can happen more naturally and sustainably.

4.

Needs and wants

Are you clear about what you want in a loving relationship? What do you believe will make you happy and satisfied with your life? What are your plans and hopes for the future?

Keep a clear vision of a healthy relationship close to your heart.

It's OK to talk with friends about these dreams and hopes. But they may respond with ideas about themselves, not necessarily ideas that are right for you.

You may find your needs and wants will change and grow as time passes. Be prepared for change, and review your vision regularly.

5.

What do they want?

Once you have spent time working out your vision for a healthy relationship, welcome the opportunity to talk about your needs and desires with your partner.

It's impossible to understand what goes on in someone else's mind. Trying to second guess what they want, without asking them is hopeless. You can't possibly know what they want from a relationship.

Few people are very confident about falling in love or have developed ideas about what they want. When you and the other person discuss your needs for a healthy relationship, you become clearer, and so does the other person.

Don't be afraid to ask them what they want.

6.

Perspective

At different times in your life, you can easily believe things that are not real or true for you. Other people's ideas will influence you. Ideas can come into your mind that seem to be OK at the time but later you might ask yourself: *Why did I think like that?* or *Why did I do that?*

Find ways to keep connected with what's real and true for you. *Are you clear about what you're thinking and believing? Are there any little things that worry you at the moment? Are any of your family or friends asking you distressing questions?*

Talking with someone you trust can help you put things into perspective. Ask your partner, a friend, or a family member to sit with you and listen while you talk about your challenges. A human listening post can help you to hear yourself clearly and you will be able to solve most of your issues yourself, just from being heard properly.

Encourage honesty within yourself. Don't expect others to be honest with you if you are not honest with them. Find a way to keep in touch with what's real for you.

7.

The gift of being on your own

Learn how to enjoy being in your own company. You can learn so much about yourself when you spend time alone, listening to your thoughts. Invest in some time alone to get to know yourself better — to know yourself as you would a close friend.

If you look for a relationship to fill an empty space within you, it won't make you happy for long. The other person may not be who or what you think they are, or you may not be who or what they want.

If that space in you is filled with caring for yourself, then when you do find someone to love, the relationship can start from strength and equality rather than needing and wanting someone to make you happy.

If you already like yourself, the other person liking or loving you is a bonus.

Even if you are happy in a relationship, take some time to be alone to maintain your self-care.

8.

Appreciate yourself first

Your needs and feelings are important. It takes time and effort to get to know yourself well.

Think about what you want and how you feel. Take care that you do not let your thoughts and actions about another person pull you ahead of getting to know yourself first. The more you know and like yourself, the more chance your relationship has of success.

Your partner will want to get to know who you are, so it's important to have taken the time to work that out, to be clear about who you are and what you want. When you share this with another person, they will be meeting the real you, the authentic you.

9.

Trust yourself

Free will is the capacity to decide by yourself for yourself. Your judgement and experience will guide you to use your free will.

By listening to your inner thoughts and feelings you will build trust within yourself. This will improve your confidence to make the best judgements for yourself at any moment.

Using free will is like exercising your body. If you don't exercise your body, you will lose some of your strength, and your body may not work as well as it could. Free will needs to be used every day for it to be a strength in your life.

10.
Fate

Predetermined by a supernatural power, fate is often described as being bigger or more important than free will. It is often used to explain things that feel destined to happen — an event that appears to be out of your control.

Fate can lead to happy relationships sometimes, sometimes not. Some people leave their lives up to fate, including their love lives. Others believe they control their lives through free will.

> *When I met him, I knew it was fate. I wasn't meant to be at the bus stop. It wasn't a bus stop I have ever been to before. I was there because I was late and a friend dropped me there to catch my bus, and I started talking to this man because he was also waiting. That's how I met my boyfriend, fate bought us together. So, the relationship must have been meant to happen.*
>
> Tuck

Fate may draw you together in the first place but your free will to act and react in healthy ways will be what keeps you together.

Falling In Love

When I saw you first,
it took every ounce of me not to kiss you.

When I saw you laugh,
it took every ounce of me not to fall in love.

And when I saw your soul —
it took every ounce of me.

Atticus

11.

The dream of romance

The idea of romantic love is a strongly held belief in most people. The dream of someone coming into your life, falling in love with them, and everything is wonderful forever.

The dream of falling deeply in love and living happily ever after is common amongst both men and women. This is not how it happens most of the time. Love can be difficult and painful at times, and it takes work and effort to sustain a loving relationship.

Once the first romantic stage in a relationship has passed, a different kind of love can emerge. However, you may grieve those first romantic feelings and not be able to commit to a different kind of love. Some people keep changing partners because they only want to feel that first romantic falling in love feeling.

Most people in long-term relationships still enjoy flutters of romantic feelings from time to time, where that first falling in love feeling returns for short periods. Often on a holiday or when something out of the ordinary has happened.

Falling in love is just the first step in a relationship, not the whole of it. Have the courage to accept that love changes, so that deeper love and contentment can emerge.

12.

Being present

There is no special way to love someone, everyone has their unique way to express this. However, some people find it difficult to open their hearts to love. They don't want to be hurt, so they hold back their feelings.

I was always fearful of opening myself up to love. I had seen my mother get hurt over and over again as I was growing up, and I didn't have much trust in relationships. So, when I met someone I liked, I would hold my feelings back, and they saw this as me not being interested in them and walked away from me and any kind of relationship with me. It's still hard for me to just be open and take a chance.

Janelle

Being in the moment with that special person, like smiling and being present for them is a great start. Opening your heart to the other person gives the relationship a chance to grow and develop.

13.

Open your heart

Many people are afraid to open their heart to trust another person just in case they are misunderstood or hurt. They are afraid that the stakes are too high, and there's always the risk that if they love someone, they will be rejected.

What's does it feel like to open your heart to someone?

> *Opening my heart happens when my four-year-old niece comes running up the stairs with a big smile on her face. I see her and my heart fills with love, joy, and happiness. That to me is opening my heart. To just feel present, open, and loving and not expect anything in return.*
>
> Adrienne

Opening your heart to love another person takes courage. There is always the risk that love will not work out and you will be hurt, but falling in love without opening your heart is like having sushi without wasabi. One doesn't work without the other.

14.

Your intuition

It can be difficult when you are falling in love to keep your mind clear and open to hear your inner wisdom.

Love can make it difficult for you to make up your mind about what to do and what not to do. Sometimes you will want to ask someone else about what you should do. If you do this, remember that mostly they will tell you what they would do in the same situation.

Let's say you tell a friend you want to live with your boyfriend and you are leaving home to do this. For them, it may seem to be the worst choice in the world and a very stressful choice, so they advise you not to do it. This is them talking about their fears and their worries.

They might say, *'You are doing the wrong thing, moving in with him,'* or the seed of doubt advice, *'Are you sure you know what you're doing?'* What they really mean to say is, *'The thought of doing this makes me feel uneasy because I couldn't do it, so it scares me to talk about it.'*

Their view, not yours.

Listen to your feelings and intuition, these will guide you to solve your issues and problems. Trust and listen to the advice from others, but always make your own decisions by following your inner wisdom.

15.

Create with passion

Passion can easily be lost when you get used to each other in a relationship. Talking, listening, and spending time together are all ways to reconnect with the passion you felt at the start.

Connect with your passion by having more fun, and by being warm and close. Share your thoughts of love, think kindly about yourself and them, listen attentively, and be caring for your partner.

Spend time, money, and energy on experiences, rather than on things. When you engage in activities together, you learn more about how you can interact with each other.

Touch more, laugh more, and do things for the other person they are not expecting. This is how you create more passion in your life.

16.

Love takes time

It takes time to get to know another person well.

The person you fall in love with may not be the type of person you would have expected to fall for. Make the time to get to know them first before you choose to be with them forever. Don't rush into a serious relationship too fast.

The other person may be getting used to their feelings that may be new to them. They may need time and attention to settle into their emotions.

When you take your time to get to know someone well, it helps a deep friendship to grow and gives your relationship a better chance of success.

17.

Reality check

How do you check that your relationship is what you think it is?

When you're first in love, it's very easy not to notice things about the other person that you may not like. Love has a way of making you blind to the other person's faults.

When love is new, strong, and passionate, it's hard to stop and check your feelings deeply. If your thoughts become unclear and you don't know if your relationship is right for you, this is the time to give yourself a reality check.

> *I was so in love I just went along with everything my boyfriend wanted. I had a small feeling that something wasn't right in our relationship but I just didn't want to look too closely for fear it may unravel. As it turned out, he had a wife and child in another town and I was just a bit of fun to him.*
>
> Tabitha

When you take the time to listen, you will notice any red flags about the other person that could be overlooked in the heat of passion. Ask the hard questions to get to know that person.

18.

Pace your feelings

When you rush into a relationship, you may not see the other person as they really are. You may lose contact with your values. Everyone needs time to think about their desires first; to be clear about what they value in a relationship.

Pace your feelings towards the other person until you have worked out what is important to you. This can be hard to do because passion can be so very strong, and you may not want to go slowly.

The difficulty is that if you yourself are not clear about your needs, you cannot be clear with the other person about these needs.

It's essential to balance passion with getting to know yourself first.

New Love

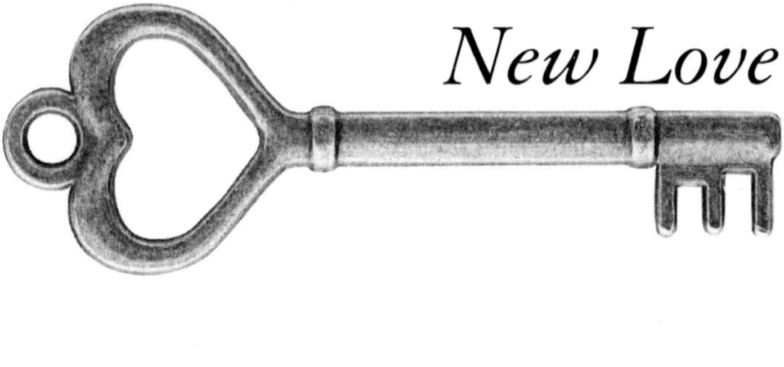

New love is grand.
Savour all the crazy, muddled might of it.

Eli Easton

19.

Listen to understand

Everyone is different. There are no two people who have the same likes or dislikes. Each person's life is completely different from everyone else's.

Your partner will probably have had a very different life from yours. Sometimes that's what bought you together in the first place. Try to imagine what their life has been like and appreciate where they have come from.

The only way you can learn about another person is to communicate with each other. If you feel that something is not quite right, ask questions and discuss how you can go forward together with a better understanding of each other.

When you listen to someone with all your attention, you will understand them better and they will respect you more. They in turn may listen to you more when you choose to speak.

20.

Grow the friendship

When you are in love and especially when love is new, you may feel that life is moving quickly and everything is rushing forward. There can be much excitement in your heart and mind, and this is great. But it's very easy to let this excitement carry you along without thinking about where the relationship is going and exactly what you want from it.

When this happens to you, think about what you and your partner can do to grow the relationship together. Think about asking your partner to discuss and plan things together and find shared goals.

Let them know about the things that are important to you. Help them to get to know you, and learn how to ask for support for your needs. Talk together about how you can grow the friendship between you.

These things will help you and your partner to nurture your relationship.

21.

Nurture trust

Trust between two people can grow through getting to know each other and dealing with difficult things together. Talking through events that are hard to deal with builds this trust between people.

It's natural to try to hide some of the murkier things about yourself from your partner. You might want to keep quiet about the parts of you that might show you in a bad light, or show you to be weak.

You will lessen your partner's trust if you hide these things from them. They will sense that you are keeping something important from them, and this will diminish their trust.

Be open with your partner about the things that are hard for you to share, as well as the things that are easy to share. Make a habit of listening to them about the things that are hard for them to deal with.

22.

Choose the outcome

How many times have you said, *He made me feel bad* or *She made me feel sad?* No one can make you feel anything without your permission. You choose how you react to what has been said. The other person can't make you feel it, you do.

People feel good or bad because of what they say to themselves about what another person has said.

If your partner says, *'I don't like what you are wearing.'* You can think, *Well that's their point of view but I like it and I am going to wear it.* Or you can think, *Why do they want to hurt me, they don't love me or truly care about me.*

Two very different ways of thinking about what your partner has said. The first reflects that they can have that point of view but you don't share it. The second is unkind and hurtful and is not necessarily true.

It's what you say to yourself about what the other person has said, that hurts the most, not what is said.

23.
Being cheerful

Remember to enjoy yourself, to have fun, to be light and cheerful most of the time.

There are times when you might not feel happy and times when you have things to think or worry about. You might have to work hard for a while or focus strongly on a project or job. It's still possible to be happy and light within yourself even though you have deadlines.

There are many opportunities when you could choose to be lighter and more cheerful. This will help to keep your spirit strong, and more able to get along with others when times are hard.

Being light and happy makes any interaction with your work colleagues, family, and friends more pleasant. Sharing your fun and happiness with your partner can add to the enjoyment for both of you.

You can choose to be more cheerful and to have more fun.

24.

Ask questions

Show genuine interest when you ask about your partner's values and beliefs. Don't be afraid to ask them what they feel or think.

Some people don't find it easy to ask their partner about themselves. If you are one of these people, make the effort to do this more. Ask what are you feeling, or what's happening for them. Then listen to their answer. Really listen. Don't start asking another question or make a comment, wait and listen to them with all your attention.

Learn to be a loving, listening person. When you grow your understanding of them, you will nurture the love between you.

25.

Don't jump ahead

Everyone can hold many thoughts at the same time. Jumping ahead of what is happening now occurs because you are used to multitasking. You can think about many things at once, including thinking about the future. But over-thinking about the future will not support what you are doing right now.

> *I am always thinking about tomorrow and when the day is over, I feel unhappy because I haven't done much. I think it's because I think too much about tomorrow and not enough time about what I am doing right now.*
>
> Henry

Be aware and enjoy the present moment. Give it your best, rather than going too far forward in time.

26.

Be yourself

Sometimes people act differently than they are. Don't pretend that you're someone you're not. It can be very hard to keep this up, and you do yourself a great disservice.

Your values become who you are, and are very important in a relationship. Make it clear what you stand for and believe in. Act on what is true for you. If you lose who you are by not honouring your values, your relationship will struggle. You may end up resenting the other person because you are not who you really are with them. Expressing your values can help you to be more of who you truly are.

You don't have to agree with the other person's values to have a happy relationship. But you need to express your values and beliefs to give the other person the chance of understanding who you are, even if they don't agree with you.

You also need to think about how you can accept their values, even if you don't agree with all of them.

Keeping the Flame Alive

Falling in love is easy.
Falling in love with the same person repeatedly
is extraordinary.

Crystal Woods

27.

Forgive the past

Everyone finds it hard to forgive someone who has done something painful or thoughtless. It's easy to let your mind relive what they did to hurt you.

Going over it, again and again, does not help you to get on with your life. The other person might have hurt you once — but every time you think about it, you relive that same intense hurt again. By re-living the pain in your mind, you end up hurting yourself more than the person who hurt you in the first place.

Forgiveness is the ability to give up the idea that your past could have been any different. When a thought comes up about the past, where you feel shame, blame, or guilt for the part you played in it, lean into where the feeling lands in your body instead of going down a rabbit hole of blame, shame, and guilt. Lean into it, don't be afraid of the feeling, eventually, it will let go of you. Nothing could ever have been any different for your highest good, your growth, or your creativity.

The great thing about the past is that it's over.

If you have done something wrong, learn from that and try not to do it again. Forgive yourself and think about how you can be better in the future.

28.
Extended family

When you commit yourself to someone, you also commit to their ancestry. Having a relationship doesn't mean that it is with that one person alone. Your partner's family may play a very important role in their life. They have had a long relationship with them and they know each other well.

They will have established ways of talking and doing things with each other. And will have their ways to show their love for each other, which may be very different from yours.

You may even think that your partner's extended family doesn't want you in their lives and this can lead you to feelings of isolation. The thing to remember here is that they love your partner and want the best for them. Try to remain open and cheerful when you are with them.

Demonstrate that you are happy to share your partner with their family by trying to understand them. Listen to them carefully and ask them questions so you may come to know them better.

29.

Happiness goals

Most people want happy lives. They want to be happy in their relationships, their work, their friendships, and in the way they learn.

Think carefully about what you would like to achieve in your life — what do you think would help you to be happy?

Having some money and security is important, and it's valuable to have goals about these things but think across every part of your life.

Here are some daily goals for wellbeing and happiness:

- Walk, or exercise.
- Take time for yourself every day, even if it's just 15 minutes.
- Do something out of the ordinary for someone you love, remind them of their strengths, or do something kind for them.
- Do something creative for yourself — paint, dance, draw, sing or write.

Making goals for these things will help you to enjoy a balanced, happy life.

30.

Show compassion

Compassion is showing care and kindness to another person rather than being rigid, distant, or harshly judging them. By opening your heart to them, even when they have done something wrong, bad, or hurtful, demonstrates that you have a kind heart.

Don't try to help them to find an answer to their problems; only they can do that. Listening with your heart open is a compassionate response for both them and you.

Deep listening is the key to compassion. Listening, and actively hearing others can help you to better understand and think more kindly about them.

Extend compassion to yourself, as well as being kind to others.

31.

Visualise love

Love starts out being exciting, fresh, new, fun and if nurtured, can evolve into something much deeper. But it's easy to take love for granted. If this happens, there is a risk that your passion loses its energy and hope for the future.

Visualise a strong picture of your love, a mind picture of you and your partner as you would like your love to be. See yourself caring for each other, laughing together, and sharing friendship and love.

Then match your behaviour to that vision. This means doing something small every day to demonstrate this vision. A touch, a smile, going out of your way to be kind, or treating them with deep respect, are all things that will show them your love.

Keep your love fresh and alive by sharing your vision with your partner.

32.

The goal of love

Goals are important in any relationship. The best way to build your love together is to have positive goals — things you want to do together.

Goals for how you talk with each other, how much time you spend together, how you are going to grow the friendship between you, and how you are going to show your love for each other. Take time to connect and make these goals together.

Focus on what you want, rather than what you don't want. Having clear goals about the love you want helps your mind to stay clear and focused.

33.

Focus on the 80%

It's easy to place too much attention on the things that have gone wrong or have been unpleasant in a day. Human beings are hard-wired to focus on what hasn't worked.

We are born with an inherent negative bias. While this protected us as a species in the past when we needed to be wary of potential dangers to survive, our negative bias triggers us to be unconsciously focused on what's going wrong, what's missing, and what might go wrong in the future.

The things that haven't worked are only a small part of the overall picture, probably less than 20%. If you speak mostly about these mistakes, this is how you'll believe life is.

What about the other 80% that's OK? Do you give this enough thought or consideration?

Make sure you talk positively about the 80% positive when it happens. You will feel lighter and happier and the world will seem a much better place.

34.

Tell the truth

In any relationship it's important to be honest with each other, to tell the truth.

Most of us were taught to be nice people, to be peace*keepers*, not peace*makers*. Being nice at the cost of suppressing our real thoughts and feelings doesn't get us anywhere. Being nice usually means the abandonment of self. This is not our collective fault, but changing it is our individual responsibility.

If you say that everything is fine when it isn't, you might think that you are being kind to your partner but instead, you are not being fair to them or yourself. And next time they ask you about something, they may question whether you are trying to be nice, or whether they can trust your answer.

Tell the truth with kindness but tell the truth.

35.

Ask for the truth

Sometimes your partner will say things to be pleasant or kind to you, rather than being truthful.

You might ask if they like something you want to buy. If they're truthful, they will say yes, or no. If they are trying to please you, they might say that it's great, when it clearly isn't.

Which would you rather hear?

Talk to your partner about being truthful with you every time, even if it's not what your ego likes to hear.

The key is then not to react badly if they tell you something you don't like.

36.

Let go of control

Most people do not like being told what to do.

When you tell someone what to do, you are controlling them, rather than wanting the best for them.

Controlling another person's actions and thoughts by trying to get them to do or think differently will not be successful in the long term.

When one person tries to control the other, it creates tension in the relationship. One person may be happy but the other is unhappy. This is not a solution for a resilient relationship.

Ask for the things you need in a relationship without trying to control what the other person says or does. This way if the person does what you ask, they do it because they are free to do it, not because you are trying to control their actions and thoughts.

It's not possible to control another person; if you try, you will make them and yourself very unhappy.

37.

Fast-track Learning

Learning is a constant in life. Everything you do gives you a chance to learn more about yourself and others.

Being in a relationship is a fast-track way to learn because when you are close to another person, they will reflect both the good and the not-so-good things about you.

When you notice what you react to, it gives you the chance to think about what you could do differently next time. And if you are brave enough, you can change the way you do things for your self-improvement.

You learn from another person by noticing your feelings and then changing the way you see and do things.

38.

Choose happiness

Everyone has the potential for happiness — of being able to look on the bright side of life.

Difficult things happen to everyone. You will have some good times and some difficult times, some good days and bad days.

When things are tough, it's an opportunity to think about fixing whatever has caused the problem. You may think about what you can do differently or better next time.

At the same time, you can choose not to over-worry about problems. Be lighter in your spirit during difficult times — both in your actions and reactions.

Choose not to think constantly about problems, think about the happy things in your life, and be grateful for these happy times. Gratitude always builds more things to be grateful for.

You can choose to look for happiness even when things are difficult.

39.

Small acts of love

Doing something thoughtful, kind, or generous, always supports a healthy relationship.

Small acts of love will nurture and nourish the love between you. Like being generous with your time or attention, or writing your partner a note or a card with a message of love, or buying them a book or magazine about something that interests them. These things do not have to cost a lot of money to be valued, and will demonstrate that you are thinking about them.

This thoughtfulness will show them how much you care for them.

40.

Tender touch

One of the things that babies and children value is the sense of touch. Being touched is as important to them as their sense of well-being and safety. As you grow up, this wonderful part of your life — touching, and being touched — may not happen as often. Adults can grow out of the habit of touch.

Touch your partner often. A gentle touch on the arm or a soft touch to the face demonstrates kindness and connection. It talks to both of you about your love and helps the well-being of your relationship.

Hold hands. Sit closely when watching TV or screens, or when you are relaxing together.

You may not be aware of how much a gentle touch can help you build your love and appreciation of each other. Your heart will recognize this touch and this will add to building a deep love between you.

41.

Listen carefully

Your mind can bring up thoughts and pictures much faster than you can speak words. This is one reason you might find it hard to listen fully when another person is talking.

It's very easy to start thinking ahead while another person is speaking. Your mind can hold many ideas at one time. It can think about what you'll have for lunch and what you'll do when you get back to work. It's not unusual to think of what you might say next, after the other person has finished, and it's your turn to speak.

Thinking too far ahead shows a lack of respect for the other person. Listen carefully to understand the other person, this will show you have consideration for them.

The other person can sense if you are not listening carefully. When you listen with care, it helps to build a close and positive relationship.

Take special care to listen to your partner.

42.

Be friends

Love is the base for a successful relationship and friendship is the nourishment that helps the relationship to grow and be healthy. Friendship and love are the balance that strengthens a relationship and helps it to stay strong.

Love comes from a deep sense of togetherness and the joining of two souls. It's mostly about your feelings, whereas friendship is very much about how you both get along together, and what you are prepared to do to nourish that connection.

Learning about the other person builds this friendship, by listening, being thoughtful, being helpful, being kind, and caring.

Remember to keep your friendship as an essential part of your relationship, which supports your love.

43.

Inner wisdom

When things aren't working in your relationship and it doesn't feel right, listen to your inner wisdom. Here are some ideas you can apply:

- Breathe deeply and listen to what's happening inside of you.
- Ask yourself, *What is the best thing for me to do right now?*
- Let go and wait for an idea or thought to come. It might take minutes or days, but an answer will come.
- Be alert and look for answers around you; you may just feel a small understanding of what to do next.
- You may be talking with someone and they will say something that answers your question.
- Act upon these small understandings, do what you believe needs to be done.

When you move into your inner wisdom, you move your awareness beyond the analytical mind and connect to a world of thoughts and feelings. This part of you knows things that your thinking mind does not see or know.

Trust yourself because, no matter what advice you receive from other people, it's you that has to deal with your life and your relationships.

44.

Small things

It's easy to be hurt by your partner over minor incidents. Thinking too much about these can make you very unhappy. If you are not careful, negative feelings about these experiences can be what you think about most of the time.

Don't spend too much time fixating on these small things that are niggling you about your partner. Balance this by thinking about what you like and love about them as well. There will be much more of these.

Think about three things they do that are kind or supportive of you and write them in your diary or journal. This will help to balance the negatives with the good things they do.

And learn to accept the small things because this is what they are … small things.

45.

Ups and downs

You mislead yourself if you think you should always feel loving towards your partner as you did at the beginning. Ordinary life will have an impact on your feelings, as everyday living takes your attention.

Be loving and gentle with yourself when you feel distanced from your partner. Think about the dreams you had at the start of your relationship to remind you of your shared vision of love.

It is healthy to have ups and downs in your emotional life. Having kind thoughts towards yourself will help you get back on track with your shared vision.

46.

Dreams can come true

Visualisation is a powerful tool in matters of the heart. Build a clear picture in your mind of the love you feel for your partner. Imagine what you like about them, such as their strengths and abilities.

Keep this picture in the front of your mind, even if it's not what's happening in your life right now. Having this clear picture of what you want in your relationship, plus the way you behave with your partner, is a powerful way to create your vision of love.

Dream about your future with as much love and happiness as you can. Expect the best from love and believe that this dream can come true.

47.

Accept the differences

If you and your partner have different ideas and beliefs, then you are like most people in relationships. It's normal to have beliefs and thoughts that are very different from your partner's.

It's easy to get caught up with the thoughts and beliefs that you don't share, rather than all the thoughts and beliefs you share. There are probably more of these than you think.

Accept that the differences between people add to the pleasure and richness of life. Look at the ideas and beliefs you share and build on these. This is the way a relationship can grow and become stronger, which leads to building a healthier and deeper love.

48.

Balanced feedback

Balance the way you talk with your partner. Think and talk about the optimistic things you see them doing and saying. If you only talk with them about all the things they don't do well, it will break the bond of love between you, and the relationship will fall apart.

Build a strong bond with your partner by talking about the things that are working well most of the time.

When you talk about the things that are not working, do this in a way that is compassionate and kind. And don't sandwich your feedback by putting a positive in with a negative, they didn't happen together, so don't link them together. This message will confuse the other person.

Give positive feedback when good things happen, don't save it up. The same goes for things you are unhappy about. The closer to the event you tell them, the more authentic it will be.

Take care to balance the way you talk with your partner.

49.

Grow your love

Love never stays the same, it changes all the time. All relationships need work and care to develop and grow.

Sometimes your relationship feels great, sometimes it feels like it's all wrong. You won't learn or grow unless something is uncomfortable. Be kind to yourself and your partner during times of discomfort and growth.

Practise the things you need to grow your love, such as talking, listening, and showing your love for each other.

You and your partner can live through hard times, growing together and learning to love each other more as time passes.

Love will evolve as it changes.

Throughout It All

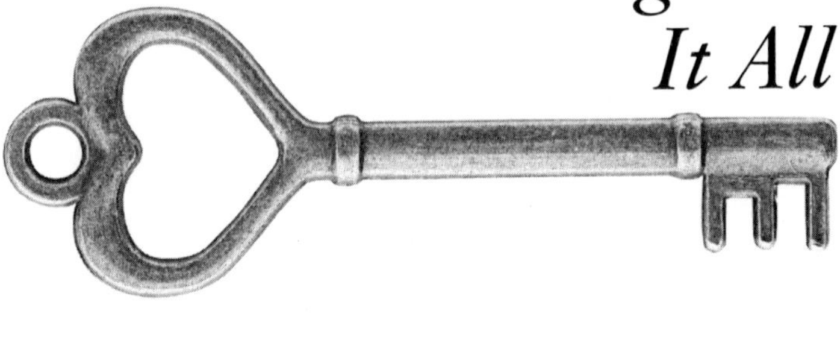

A great marriage is not when the perfect couple comes together. It is when an imperfect couple learns to enjoy their differences.

Dave Meurer

50.

Learn from everything

Positive events in your life can make you feel happy but not for long because these are absorbed quickly. You learn the least from happy events as they are the least difficult. You learn the most from experiences that challenge you.

It's the negative and difficult events that make you stronger. They allow you to think about how you do things and how you could do them differently next time.

When things go wrong, you can be angry and blame yourself, or blame the other person or situation. Blaming yourself or others over what has happened in the past is unkind. Think about what you might learn from difficult events and people, and how you can change for the better.

Forgiving yourself for the past means that you are giving up the hope that things could have been any different.

51.

Choices for anger

Everyone has events which happen to them that can leave them feeling angry and upset.

For example, if you feel that you have done a good job but are treated badly at work, you have three choices.

1. You can believe that it's not fair, and dislike whoever has treated you badly by being angry with them, which leads to feeling like a victim of the situation.
2. You can try to understand that sometimes things happen that are unpleasant, and whatever happened is past.
3. Or can choose to learn from the experience, then move on with your life.

There is no value in staying angry. Move on and be pleased with yourself for understanding that life is about learning, not about who is right and who's wrong.

The choice is to be strong and learn, or to be sad and feel sorry for yourself. You make that choice.

52.

A safe place

A loving relationship offers the opportunity for two people to understand each other better, and to understand themselves better. This close relationship can become a safe place to learn.

New experiences give you plenty of chances to learn and grow your skills and knowledge. You can help each other to understand the things that happen to you and what lessons can be learnt.

With your partner, agree that you can talk to each other equally about your experiences, share what you have learnt, and decide together what happens next.

The amount of friendship and trust that can be created between two people in a close relationship is endless.

53.

Difficult times

All relationships have difficulties at times. Sometimes this means that love is over, but mostly it means that you have an opportunity to make changes together to allow both of you to grow.

Think carefully about what has triggered your unhappiness. Writing in your diary or journal helps crystallise your feelings and needs. Then talk with each other about your collective needs, and be willing to listen and be open to what comes from the discussion.

Be prepared for change, but also be prepared for you and your partner to do things differently to work towards happiness again.

54.

Blame game

When difficult times arise, it's easy to be diverted to blaming yourself, rather than thinking constructively about what part you have played in it. Be truthful but don't over-state your part. Diving into blame, shame, or guilt will not solve it, and will take away from your self-esteem.

If you blame your partner for all of the problems in the relationship, you will lose any chance of you both talking through the issue. The truth is that one person alone is never responsible for a problem between two people. Problems arise with each person playing some part in creating it.

Recognise that you have added something to whatever difficulties you are having. Accept that you can talk with your partner about these issues as a step along the path of growing together

55.

Don't hold back

Everyone has an inbuilt gift for caring and showing love but some people hold back their love.

They may have had experiences in the past where they have been hurt. They may not have been able to show love in the past and need time to build trust with you, to allow them to open their hearts.

It's important to love openly, even if you feel you are not receiving the love you desire.

Talk with your partner about how you feel, and explain how you would like to be treated. Ask the same from them.

This will demonstrate that you care for both yourself and them.

56.

You can't please everyone

We are all busy with our lives, and it can be hard to please everyone. Doing your work well, having a happy relationship, relaxing, and spending time with friends and family is hard to do all at once. Sometimes this can lead to stress.

It's best to have some very clear ideas about what you want for yourself and follow these, rather than trying to be all things to everyone else. When you try to make everyone happy, you will wear yourself out and make yourself miserable.

Remember to listen to your own beliefs and values and follow these. Work out what you believe in and follow that every day. If you do this, you will be less stressed and a happier, more honest person.

57.

Adapt to change

It's easy to think that your partner will stay the same as they were when you first met. Change happens to everyone at different times and different stages in the relationship.

Adapting to change is something you need to do as your love grows. This means being able to see the changes that are happening around you and keeping an open mind to doing things differently.

Relationships usually start with lots of things that you both like about each other. When things change, it's easy to forget why you liked each other at first. Try to remember the good things every day, and share these with your partner.

This helps to nurture the relationship in a very meaningful way.

58.

Stay connected

Throughout your relationship, it's important to stay connected to your feelings. Take notice and think about your feelings without being hurt or upset.

Your feelings will always help you to understand what is happening in your world and your relationships. They are very useful in telling you if something is or isn't right. Let them connect you to what is happening around you.

Sit gently with these feelings and carefully listen to them, take note of where they land in your body. Honour these feelings by staying in this discomfort, without attaching a story about who's right and who's wrong, while consciously breathing.

When the balance of what is happening has tipped in some way, don't be frightened by your feelings, meet them with compassion and kindness. Close your eyes and rest into your feelings and eventually, they will let go of you.

Resistance to discomfort only causes more anxiety. Sometimes you'll decide to act upon your feelings, sometimes you will just notice them and feel kindness for allowing yourself to feel them.

59.

You are enough

Look after yourself physically and emotionally by letting go of trying to gain approval from other people. Your value is not someone else's decision. If you find yourself wanting approval from others, begin by giving yourself the approval you seek from them.

Sit quietly, focus on your heart and breathe in as you say the following: *I am enough, I have enough, I do enough*. Then exhale. Repeat this three times and notice how you become more relaxed with each breath.

60.

Present time

When you think too much about a problem, it can turn to worry in a heartbeat. The things you worry about may have happened days ago but you're still worrying about them now.

The key is to let go of thoughts about the past and live in present time. Remind yourself of what you are doing now. You may be sitting in a chair, on a train, at work, or sitting at home. Wherever you are right now is important. Try to bring yourself back to what's happening now, in this moment.

Redirect your thoughts to being grateful for what you have, not beating yourself about what you don't have. Be thoughtful about how you speak to yourself about yourself. Be aware of negative thinking about the past, or anxiety about the future, as it can be very painful.

Draw yourself back into the present moment by searching out three things you can see or focus on. Notice three things you can smell and three things you can touch. This helps you to concentrate on what's working in your life now.

No one can change the past. Forgive yourself for thinking that your past could have worked out any differently. Let go of what you said or did yesterday and look at where and what you are doing right now.

The great thing about the past is, it's over.

61.

You can't change someone else

Many people start a relationship thinking they can fix someone else or make another person better in the way they want them to be.

This does not work.

Don't ever believe that asking someone to change will make them change, it won't. If someone else is ready to change, they will change because they want to, not because someone else has asked them to.

People change because what they are doing is so uncomfortable or hurtful to them that they have to find a better way to do it.

Change the things about yourself you can change, and love and accept your partner as they are.

62.

Self-care is a strength

Do you care for yourself well, or do you see that another person's needs are more important than your own? When you care for yourself first, you will have more energy to care for another person in a relationship.

Self-care has the same rule as the safety instructions on an aeroplane — first, give yourself oxygen before assisting another.

Caring for yourself well is a strength, not a weakness.

Just because you can do so much for another person, doesn't mean you should. Learn to live with the discomfort and disappointment from others, as you learn to take care of yourself. Sometimes this means saying no to someone you love.

Your first love needs to be of self, without that, you have very little to give.

63.

Keep energy for yourself

Living a busy life and having so many things that need your attention can weaken your energy levels.

If you feel like your energy is getting low, here are some ideas you can try to keep your energy strong and vibrant:

- Find time to be by yourself, for yourself.
- Say no if you have too much to do.
- Ask for help when you need it.
- Make a list of all the good things about yourself and read it every day for a month.
- Work out something you enjoy doing and make time to do it every day, even if just for half an hour.
- Have more sleep or relaxation.

Any of these things will help you to generate strong positive energy for yourself.

64.

Choose friends carefully

Not everyone is healthy to be around. If your trust and friendship are not returned, you will feel on some level that the relationship is out of exchange, which means one person contributes more than the other. Observe how you feel about yourself after you've been with them — if you feel uncomfortable or upset, that's a clear indication that something is out of balance in the relationship.

You can talk with them first to try to clear things up between you. But if they continue to be dishonest and unsupportive of you, make the decision to stop spending time with them.

If you hold on to a friendship when you can't trust the friend, you are likely to bring hurt and pain to yourself, and your self-esteem will be affected. You may think that you should accept them as they are and give them another chance, but to do so will lessen your self-value and can invite more pain.

It can be a very hard decision to make, especially if you have been friends for a long time. But you can move away from a friendship quietly, without making a fuss.

65.

Unhealthy relationships

Have you ever walked away from a friend and felt badly? Felt like something the other person did or said wasn't very nice or didn't feel right?

Sometimes friendships change and your friends may not have your best interests at heart. They may feel jealous of what you have or what they think you have.

Trust your feeling that something is not quite right. Sometimes you have to let go of a past friendship because it is not healthy for you anymore.

I loved my friend Sak, but she was so jealous of my life with my boyfriend and my job, we just didn't have any fun together. I miss her but I had to stop seeing her as it was poisoning my life. It was just not easy to be with her anymore, she became so cruel.

Lucy

Loving Yourself

Love is not something we give or get; it is something that we nurture and grow, a connection that can only be cultivated between two people when it exists within each one of them — we can only love others as much as we love ourselves.

Brené Brown

66.

Trust the way you look

When you think about your body, are you kind about it? Or are you unkind to yourself about your body or how you look?

Do you think you should be taller, more attractive, thinner, or have a different shape? If you don't like yourself now because of the way you look, you may not like yourself any better if you were able to change.

Acceptance is the key, learn to like all the things about yourself as you are now, your imperfections included. This is a strong step forward in self-care.

Change what you can change by setting small goals. Be realistic and consistent with the action you take. If it's changing your fitness, start walking for 15 minutes a day and build on this every week. If it's your health, choose something you will take away from your eating habits, and something you will add, and do this regularly.

Be kind on your journey of self-care, don't beat yourself up if you don't achieve this every day. Be gentle with yourself.

67.

Don't compare yourself with others

The media constantly report about the wealth and beauty of rock stars, celebrities, and actors. Collectively, we look up to these people because newspapers, social media, and websites are full of stories and pictures about these *perfect* people with *perfect* bodies and lives.

Do you believe these stories?

It's too easy to feel like a failure if you measure yourself against others.

You may also think that the people you know — friends or work colleagues, are more attractive or smarter than you.

You are unique, no one is like you. Whatever you are right now, is you.

Learn to accept and like yourself rather than being unkind to yourself by measuring yourself against other people.

68.

Be optimistic

It's healthy to think and feel optimistic about yourself. However, circumstances can take you from this feeling in an instant.

Here is some action you can take to regroup and to feel more positive about yourself:

- Accept that you are not perfect and you never will be, nor will anyone else.
- Look at what you already do well, the many things that are good about you.
- Be grateful for the good things already in your life.
- Don't think about the future or the past too much.
- Have a dream for the future but live now.
- Forgive quickly. You will eventually, so why not now?
- Care for yourself and others.
- Meet new people and make friends.
- Be kind and nurture yourself.

How can you expect others to feel optimistic about you if you are not turning up for yourself?

Learn to laugh more and play; have fun with your partner and friends.

69.

Mistakes are how you learn

Everyone makes choices that sometimes don't work out for them. We all fall short of our goals and aspirations, that's how we learn.

When you make a mistake, the most important thing is not to be too unkind to yourself. Learn from these lapses in judgment, and use *everything* that happens to you as your source of wisdom. Think, everything happens *for* me, not *to* me.

When you notice you have slipped up, take responsibility for your part in it, and the learning it provides, then move forward. Forgive yourself and absorb what to do and what not to do next time.

That's the gift mistakes can give you. The gift of education and wisdom; about yourself and about what you can do better and more wisely in the future.

70.

Don't beat yourself up

What do you say to yourself when you make a mistake? Is it mostly kind and encouraging, as it would be if you were talking to a friend who made a mistake? Or is what you say to yourself negative, hurtful, and unduly harsh?

Everyone makes mistakes; this is how you learn about yourself, and how to function in the world.

Learning to love yourself when you make mistakes is one of the most important things you will ever do. Mistakes can make you a more understanding and compassionate person.

Be open to learn from mistakes so you may grow as a person.

71.

Time for yourself

Our work culture has placed a high value on paid work. Everyone works longer hours at their everyday jobs, so it may not feel natural to spend time by yourself for yourself.

The mantra, *I work longer hours than you do,* has become a competitive sport. Some people make their relaxation time as busy as a workday. They fit in so much they never seem to stop doing things, either at work or in their own time.

Allow quiet time by creating pockets of peacefulness where you do things just for yourself. This is a very healthy way to show respect for yourself.

72.

Do you stress too much?

Do you feel stressed out by worrying about things that you can do nothing about? Or feel unduly negative at times? Or worry about work, family, and friends? Are you afraid to meet new people, or do you worry about the future?

When these thoughts arise, there are steps you can take to help yourself stay calm:

- Focus on the good things that happen around you, not just the negative things.
- Think of one small, optimistic thought at a time, and repeat this several times a day.
- Relax your thinking as well as your body.
- Talk with someone you trust about your feelings and fears.
- Write a journal or a diary about how you feel.
- Think mostly about the present, not the past or the future.
- Exercise more, or walk every day.
- Be grateful for what you have.

These are all good ways to start feeling better about yourself and less stressed.

73.

Nurture a healthy self-image

Your self-image is how you see yourself. This is different from how you feel about yourself, which is self-esteem. Is your self-image fair about the whole of you — your ability at work, how you look, your relationship skills, energy levels, goals, friendliness, and your compassion?

No one is perfect, but you are mostly capable. You have good skills in your work; some good relationships skills and you can talk clearly, listen and achieve your goals.

You may not fit the popular magazine image but you can still dress well, and present yourself acceptably to the world. While there may be a few things you would like to change about yourself, you are probably more OK than you think you are.

Think about your strengths, the things you are good at, rather than talking badly to yourself about any small thing you could have done better.

74.

Build your self-esteem

Building your self-esteem is something that needs to be nurtured daily. To help you develop realistic self-esteem, write two lists. One with your strengths and one with your weaknesses, or the things you would like to change or improve.

When you start, the weaknesses list is likely to be longer than the strengths. But when you carefully think about yourself, you will be surprised to find there are many more strengths than you originally thought.

Don't overlook small contributions. It's a strength to be able to work well, keep your home or your room organised, be a good friend to someone, or be kind to a pet.

Thinking about these strengths every day builds healthy and realistic self-esteem, which will help you to feel good about yourself.

Be clear and strong about your skills and about what you *can* do.

75.

Speak up

The things you hear from others, and the words you speak to yourself, all make a difference to your self-image, and your thoughts.

If you hear negative things all the time, you are more likely to become negative in your thinking and your actions. If you often say harsh or unkind things about others, you are likely to become harsh and unkind in your heart.

You can control your thoughts by thinking about what you say. You also can influence how people speak to you.

If people around you say harsh or unpleasant things to you, you have three choices:

1. You can ask them to change what they are saying.
2. You can stop listening to them.
3. You can leave.

You will be a stronger and better person when you choose to protect yourself from unkindness.

76.

Don't shoot the messenger

When someone tells you something, there are two parts to the message you hear. The first part is what is said, the second is what you think and feel at the time about the person who brings the message.

There is a saying which originates from battles fought a long time ago — *don't shoot the messenger*. When a message was delivered with bad news, the General would have the messenger shot so that the soldiers would not find out about the bad news before he was prepared to break it.

If you do not like the message, try not to place all your attention on the person giving it. Focus on the message itself by being more curious.

Think about what you can learn from the message; the useful parts. Sometimes the message isn't about you at all, or it may be completely wrong. It may express the feelings of the person who brought it to you, rather than being something about you.

Try to think about which part of the information can be useful to you, and leave the rest alone. Don't shoot the messenger by blaming and judging them harshly.

77.

Learn to like yourself

Many people think that the love of another person will make them happy.

Some people fear being alone because they see it as shameful. Don't bully, guilt, or shame yourself. As soon as you feel yourself *should-ing* yourself around, talk to yourself in a kind, supportive and nurturing way. You are much stronger than you think you are and could adjust quite happily to living on your own. When you learn to live with yourself and like yourself, you become much more resilient.

When you are with someone who is making you unhappy, you can also feel very alone. It's possible to be just as alone when you are with someone as without them.

It's not uncommon for people in long-term relationships to feel a deep sense of separation from others. Everything may look great on the outside but it's not unusual to feel a sense of loss, disconnection, or disorientation. It's possible to have people around and still feel lonely.

Learn to like yourself because this builds self-confidence and helps you to feel good, no matter who is or isn't in your life.

78.

Grow on your own

If you have been hurt in a relationship, being on your own can be very healing and eventually will help you to feel strong again. It will definitely give you the time and freedom to think about what you want in your next relationship.

Many people live solitary lives quite happily. Whether it's for a short time or a lifetime, it can provide a great space for you to learn, grow and figure out who you are.

Trust your perspective, your autonomy, and your choices. This is an amazing opportunity to learn and grow as a person.

79.

Connect with yourself

Part of nurturing your self-care is connecting with your inner self. This inner part of you is sometimes called inner wisdom, intuition, or inner life.

Being still is a great way to get in touch with the inner you. When you stop thinking and sit quietly, letting your mind drift, this creates a space for your inner self to breathe. It connects you to your rich inner life, a life that isn't about other people, doing things, or mainstream achievement — it's about turning up for yourself.

Each person has a unique way they can connect with this inner part of themselves. Find a way to create space and time to stop and be still, letting go of everyday life.

When I sit still and stop thinking, there is this other part of me who is just kind of happy and at ease with myself, just sitting doing nothing. This is my inner self. I feel better about myself when I make time to sit quietly. When I let go of my mind trying to make sense of everything all the time, I am a much happier person and much less stressed.

Kylie

80.

Success starts with you

Success in a relationship depends on the way you think and care about yourself, as well as how you think and care about another person.

A positive attitude about yourself is one of the most important things you can bring into your relationship. When you feel good about yourself, you can then add something strong and valuable to that relationship.

Make one small promise to yourself every day and keep it to restore self-trust. Try one of the following to get you started:

- 5 minutes of yoga.
- 5 minutes of meditation.
- 5 minutes stretching.
- 5 minutes writing a journal.
- 5 minutes sitting in nature.
- 5 minutes of reading something uplifting.

Be proud and pleased every time you keep a promise to yourself.

Being loyal and loving to yourself as well as the other person makes you a more balanced, cheerful person. When you like yourself and have a strong feeling of care and thought for yourself, you will automatically have more care and thought for other people.

81.

Your needs are important

Make time in your diary each week just for you. You can do anything you want with this time, as long as you keep it for yourself.

Unless you live away from everything, there is usually some sort of noise going on around you, even if it's just the quiet hum of a computer. Trains, cars, people, television, and loud music all make the world around you a busy place to live in.

Find a quiet place where you can be on your own. Start with sitting by yourself for two minutes a day and build this up over time.

Making space for yourself improves your sense of self-worth. When you spend time alone, your values will become clearer and more certain, and this will reinforce what you truly want in your life.

82.

Balance your needs

It's easy to care about other people's needs and forget about your own. Do you care too much about what other people ask of you and not enough about your own needs?

It's easy to believe your value is about doing things for other people, pleasing them, trying to make them like you.

Sometimes it's easier to let go of the time you had set aside for yourself and give it to someone else, because it's more comfortable than telling another person you can't help them. It may be easier for you to let their needs be more important than your own.

When you make time for yourself you will help to keep your life in balance.

83.

Self-respect

If you were your best friend, or if you were married to yourself, how long would you stay married?

To keep a positive relationship with someone, you need to be honest, trustworthy, loyal, and kind. To keep a positive relationship with yourself you need to be honest, trustworthy, loyal, and kind.

Everyone knows that to be healthy you need to look after yourself. When you put effort into being the best version of yourself, you not only care for yourself but you become a better human being.

Your thoughts, deeds, and actions have the power to heal.

You can care for yourself in many physical ways. Here are some ways you can do this:

- Listen to and respect your thoughts and feelings.
- Be kind to yourself in the way you think about yourself.
- Like yourself most of the time.
- Find ways to have fun and enjoy life.

Caring for yourself needs practise to become a life-long habit. It's completely an inside job.

84.

Self-talk

What you think about most of the time has great power in your life. You can change your thinking with how you talk to yourself. Self-talk is the ongoing conversation you have with yourself. It is present from the first waking moment in the morning until you go to sleep at night.

Self-talk also tends to be repetitive. We tell ourselves stories about what we believe happened, or what will happen. We think these stories will protect us from failure, or make us feel safe, but they are a form of avoidance.

Ensure your self-talk is mostly positive, as this contributes to you being either an optimistic or pessimistic person. Positive self-talk and behaviour develop strong self-esteem.

85.

Be careful who you spend time with

Do people around you speak badly about themselves or others when you are with them? Do they say unpleasant things about what they or others look like, or how or what they do?

Being around people like this can influence your feelings big time. If your friends don't support your values, you can choose to change who you spend time with.

It may not be easy to let go, particularly with people you are used to being with. But if they don't support the way you think and feel about yourself, you have to make that choice for your health and well-being.

86.

Speak well of your body

It's not unusual to hear a teenager and her mother speak the same way about food and exercise because they have the same beliefs about their bodies.

The same can be said about you and your friends. The way you and others speak and feel about your body has an impact on your attitude towards how you feel and look. Find the company of friends who have a healthy attitude toward their body and how they look after and care for themselves.

It's easy to reflect the values and beliefs of those you spend time with. Be with people who have a healthy relationship with food and their body. For just as your body takes good things from what you eat, you also take the views and beliefs, whether good or bad, of people you spend time with.

87.

Are you competitive?

Some people want to be better than their friends in all areas of their lives. They become competitive in sport, work, how many friends they have, how much money they spend, or the way they look.

They compete with their friends to be better than them, rather than enjoying their company.

Try to spend time with people who are not trying to be better than you. Find people who have good, balanced values, who like themselves, and like you the way you are.

88.

Move your body

Exercise is a positive way to help your body feel flexible and strong. Find exercises you enjoy that also make you feel good about yourself.

Exercise can be simple. If you catch public transport to work, get off a stop early and walk the rest of the way. Walk up the stairs instead of using the elevator or escalator. Ride a bike or walk to the shops. Practise yoga or stretching for half an hour a day. These are effective ways to exercise your body.

Practise conscious breathing as you enjoy moving your body. This encourages your body to feel well and happy.

89.

Relax

Relaxing is a big part of caring for your body.

There are other ways to relax other than watching screens. Many people go online and scroll without the thought of actually contributing anything, then they can't understand why they feel lonely instead of feeling connected. Often scrolling online triggers feelings of jealousy and anxiety.

Take time out from screens by relaxing your body.

You can relax and lessen stress by doing the following:

- Lie down.
- Close your eyes.
- Un-cross your arms and legs.
- Take some conscious, deep breaths.
- Hold each breath for a couple of seconds, then let it go.
- Allow your body to relax.
- Think about each part of your body in turn and let go of any stress you may feel in each part of your body.
- Try not to think thoughts that worry or stress you.
- Let your body feel calm.

To begin with, try this for a few minutes a day, then increase this two to three times every day.

90.

Are we there yet?

Having fun is another way to relax and enjoy yourself. This can mean doing good things like:

- Cook the food you like.
- Take a holiday.
- Clean your home and throw out things that do not bring you joy.
- Have nice things around you.
- Care for the plants in your home or office.
- Go to the movies.
- Listen to or make the music you love.
- Be kind to yourself every day.
- Read, draw, write, play, laugh, and walk more.

I love to draw pictures of trees and flowers, I'm not much good at it but it's so unlike what I do in my job all day, every day. This is my way to let go and have fun.

Callum

What do you enjoy doing? What helps you to feel lighter and happier? Find ways to do more of this in your life.

91.

Sit well and stand tall

We are all connected to our screens every day. Texts, emails, and unlimited access to these are a big part of our lives. Our screens are the gatekeeper to learning, work, and pleasure.

Screens can have a poor effect on the way you sit, and influence the way you stand. Leaning over a screen can cause stress and discomfort. When you are at a screen, remember to sit up straight, relax your shoulders and place your feet flat on the floor, don't cross your legs.

Many people have to stand for long periods during the day. Standing up straight and tall is good for your breathing and posture.

Both sitting well and standing tall are important for good health and wellness.

Good posture reflects good self-esteem.

92.

Conscious breathing

Breathing is easy, you don't have to think about it, it just happens.

Living stressful lives contributes to many people breathing short breaths into their chests but too much short breathing can leave the body in a state of fight/ flight. The quickest way to calm your body is through conscious, deep diaphragm breaths.

If you want to check how you are breathing, do the following:

- Lie down.
- Place a book on your stomach and another book on your chest.
- Take a deep breath.
- If the book on your stomach rises higher than the one on your chest you are breathing as deeply as you can.
- This is optimal breathing.

Every day, be more aware of how you breathe, especially when you are stressed or worried. Breathing deeply almost always calms your body, your mind and helps you to relax.

93.

Be grateful

When you cultivate a sense of gratitude, it builds emotional resilience and enhances your well-being.

Recognising and acknowledging good things in your life creates high levels of gratitude and is linked to life satisfaction, vitality, compassion, and hope. This stimulates a sense that your fundamental need for safety and connection is being met.

Fostering gratitude tones down the amygdala, the alarm system in your brain, and reduces the release of cortisol and adrenaline, the stress response. Frequently experiencing gratitude releases dopamine, the reward neurotransmitter. It balances out negativity, building awareness of what you want in your life, not what you don't want.

Next time you go for a walk, notice your surroundings — the leaves on the trees, rocks on the path, the colour of the sky, any experience that brings you back to mindfulness.

A morning or afternoon walk in nature helps draw soft kindness back into your body. The more grateful you are about your surroundings, the less likely you are to notice what you don't have.

Set yourself to attentive mode every time you leave the house.

When Love Is Over

If you love someone, set them free.
If they come back they're yours;
if they don't they never were.

Richard Bach

94.

Freedom of choice

There may come a time when you feel you have done everything you can in a relationship and it doesn't seem to be working.

If you have put the time and effort into your relationship and done everything you can to make it work but are always unhappy, you have three choices:

1. You can *choose* to change your thoughts about what you want from your partner and the relationship.
2. You can *accept* who and what your partner is.
3. You can *leave* the relationship.

If you are worried about your relationship, give careful thought to these three choices.

95.

Know when to leave

Everyone hopes their love will grow and they will become stronger and happier together. This doesn't always happen.

If you stay in an unhappy relationship, it's painful and can diminish your well-being. You are the only person who can look after this. Think very carefully about whether you should stay in the relationship or end it. Long-lasting sadness is painful and makes it harder for you to be happy again in the future.

If your partner is not able to talk with you honestly about your feelings, you can suggest couples counselling. If this is not an option, then caring for yourself is paramount for your well-being and mental health. Constant uncertainty feeds anxiety.

Let's not underestimate our strength and courage and our ability to change and move forward. Work out how to tell your partner it's over and make your plans to leave.

96.

Stop blaming

Many people blame and judge the person they have loved or currently love, for all the bad things that have happened in their lives. They don't stop to think that they also have added something to these events in some way.

Everyone has more control of their lives than they think they have. It can be very healing to accept that your thoughts and actions may have made your life what it is right now.

Don't blame the other person for what has or hasn't worked for you in your life. Accept the things you have both contributed to in the past, and move on.

Let go by not re-thinking the past over and over again.

Fix the things you can fix and let go of the rest. Make changes for the future by the way you think and act now. This will create the best possible future for you and your life will become much more optimistic.

97.

Steps of grief

When a relationship is over don't be surprised if you feel it quite deeply, it's easy to get lost in grief and pain. There are five stages of grief and it's sometimes hard to move from one stage to the next:

1. *This can't be happening to me*. Not yet crying or letting go. Denial by not accepting what has happened.
2. *Why me*? Feelings of anger, wanting to fight back or hurt the other person, blaming them for leaving you.
3. Making a deal for them to come back, or making deals with God to change what has happened.
4. An overwhelming feeling of sadness, loss, hurt, missing the hopes, dreams, and plans of the future.
5. Accepting the loss of the relationship. Finding the good that comes from it. Your goals are now turning towards the future.

Just being aware of where you are is a helpful way to move forward. You won't feel what you are feeling now forever. Get help if you can't work it through by yourself.

98.

When it's finally over

When a relationship is over and you accept that it cannot be brought back to life, there is pain, often there is blame. Sometimes you may blame yourself for not doing enough to keep the relationship in good health.

Time will heal this pain.

Blame is never useful; it does nothing except keep the pain of what went wrong alive in you.

Everyone can find things they could have done better, so forgive yourself for not being better or different in the past. Learn from your mistakes, these teach you to make different decisions next time.

Place your past relationship behind you. Think about your future and how you are looking forward to the new and exciting things that will come into your life.

99.

Look to the future

When a relationship is over it can be hard to go on with your life. Even if you cannot believe it right now, you will heal at some point in the future.

To feel pain after loss is normal. It proves that you are alive and that you are human. Your experience has added something to your life and will help you to look at things with more wisdom next time. In time, something good always comes from something hurtful.

When you are ready to move forward, try doing something new. You could learn a musical instrument, a new sport, or hobby. Try something you always wanted to do.

> *When I broke up with my boyfriend I started to play tennis. I always wanted to try this and never thought I had the time. I really enjoyed it and I met many people at the practise sessions. It has opened up my life again.*
>
> Souk

Breaking up with someone, whether after a month or a lifetime, can bring new chances and hope for the future.

100.

Do something kind

Taking the focus from yourself to think about others allows your body to heal.

Think about someone you know well or, not so well, and do something kind for them. You can do this so they know about it and can thank you, or you can do it without them knowing.

Here are some suggestions:

- Treat everyone as if they are part of your family.
- Share some special treats with others.
- Open the door for someone else and smile as you do this.
- Clean out all your old clothes and give them away.
- Help someone younger than you do something difficult.
- Tell your best friend you appreciate them.
- Listen carefully to others.
- Offer to do something for someone for free.

Being kind to others is also a gentle reminder to be kind to yourself. You are worthy of feeling good about yourself.

Be kind,
for everyone you meet is fighting a great battle.

Philo of Alexandria

About the Author

Vicki is an author, artist, filmmaker, writing coach, and corporate trainer. She has written 35 books and written and co-produced a documentary, *Never Forget Australia*.

Her writing career began with personal development books and has expanded to children's books, young adult, and adult fiction. Books include: *I've Found the Keys Now Where's the Car?*, *Life Smart*, *The Effective Leader*, *Signposts for Life*, *Two Pennies*, *The Little Stowaway*, *Oliver's First Big Spy Adventure*, *The Book of Hope — Antidote to Anxiety*, and *The Flying Angel*.

100 Keys of Love by Vicki Bennett and Ian Mathieson was first published in Japan in 2009. This edition has been reworked and edited for its Australian audience by Vicki Bennett.

Web: www.vickibennett.com.au
Instagram: vickibennettcreativity
Facebook: vickibennettcreativity